Lingo Dingo
and the chef
who spoke Hindi

Written by Mark Pallis
Illustrated by James Cottell

For my sons - MP

For Leo and Juniper - JC

LINGO DINGO AND THE CHEF WHO SPOKE HINDI

Story edited by Natascha Biebow, Blue Elephant Storyshaping
First Printing, 2023
ISBN: 978-1-915337-70-2
MarkPallis.com

Lingo Dingo
and the chef
who spoke Hindi

Written by Mark Pallis

Illustrated by James Cottell

NEU WESTEND
— PRESS —

This is Lingo. She's a Dingo and she loves helping.
Anyone. Anytime. Anyhow.

Lingo often helps her stylish neighbour Gunther, who lives by himself next door. She does a few jobs and has a nice chat. It makes Gunther feel good and it makes Lingo feel good too.

One day, Lingo arranged a special birthday party for Gunther. She even ordered a cake from a famous chef.

There was a knock at the door, "It must be the cake!" said Lingo.
But it was a monkey.

namaskaar. mera naam hai baavarchee nono.
" नमस्कार. मेरा नाम है बावर्ची नोनो ,
mujhe ek pareshaanee hai
मुझे एक परेशानी है ," he said.

Oh no. I can't speak Hindi yet, thought
Lingo. *Maybe ' नमस्कार ' is like 'Greetings'.*

नमस्कार = Greetings; मेरा नाम है = My name is;
मुझे एक परेशानी है = I have a problem.

" नमस्कार " said Lingo. Chef Nono replied slowly,
mujhe maaf kar do. main ek janmadin ka kek nahin bana sakata
" मुझे माफ़ कर दो. मैं एक जन्मदिन का केक नहीं बना सकता ."

"I don't understand," said Lingo. "But let me guess. You want..."

मुझे माफ़ कर दो = I am sorry;
मुझे माफ़ कर दो. मैं एक जन्मदिन का केक नहीं बना सकता = I cannot make the birthday cake

एक ट्राली = a trolley; एक खीरा = a gherkin/cucumber; गुब्बारे = balloons; नहीं = no

" मेरा ओवन टूट गया है ," explained Chef.
mera ovan toot gaya hai

" क्या मैं तुम्हारा ओवन इस्तेमाल कर सकता हूँ ?"
kya main tumhaara ovan istemaal kar sakata hoon?

Chef's oven must be broken thought Lingo. "I know!
Let's bake the cake together," she said.

मेरा ओवन टूट गया है = my oven is broken;
क्या मैं तुम्हारा ओवन इस्तेमाल कर सकता हूँ? = can I use your oven

Chef tapped his wrist. " ये वक़्त क्या है ?
ye vaqt kya hai?
nau baje? das baje?
नौ बजे? दस बजे ?" he asked.

Lingo pointed at her watch.

gyaarah baje? chalo shuroo karate hain! jaldee!
" ग्यारह बजे ? चलो शुरू करते हैं ! जल्दी !"

They only had one hour until the party.

ये वक़्त क्या है? = what time is it?; नौ बजे = nine o'clock; दस बजे = ten o'clock;
ग्यारह बजे = eleven o'clock; चलो शुरू करते हैं! = let's get started; जल्दी = quick

Chef Nono and Lingo whizzed around the kitchen:

आपके लिए एक एप्रन = an apron for you; एक कुंची = a whisk
मिक्स करने के लिए एक बर्तन. = a mixing bowl

krpaya, mujhe makkhan, cheenee,
" कृपया , मुझे मक्खन , चीनी ,
ande aur aata dena
अंडे और आटा देना ," said Chef.

Lingo wasn't sure what those words meant, so she just grabbed fish, coffee and onions instead.

machhalee, kophee aur pyaaj. ghinauna!
" मछली, कॉफी और प्याज। घिनौना !"

laughed Chef.

मक्खन = butter; चीनी = sugar; अंडे = eggs; और = and; आटा = flour; कृपया = please;
मछली = fish; कॉफी = coffee; प्याज= onions; घिनौना = disgusting

Chef plopped butter, sugar, eggs and flour into a bowl. "So that's what ' मक्खन , चीनी , अंडे और आटा ' means!" laughed Lingo.

main milaata hoon, aap milaate hain, ham milaate hain
" मैं मिलाता हूं , आप मिलाते हैं , हम मिलाते हैं ."
said Chef and together they began to mix the cake.

मैं मिलाता हूं = I mix; आप मिलाते हैं = you mix; हम मिलाते हैं = we mix

ant mein, beking paudar. do chammach

" अंत में , बेकिंग पाउडर। दो चम्मच ," said Chef. Lingo guessed

' बेकिंग पाउडर ' meant baking powder, but how much?

Before she could ask, Chef hurried away, saying,
maaf karen, mujhe thoda kaam karana hai
" माफ़ करें , मुझे थोड़ा काम करना है। "

Lingo laughed, "I can guess what ' मुझे थोड़ा काम करना है। ' means!"

अंत में = finally; बेकिंग पाउडर = baking powder; दो चम्मच = two spoonfulls;
माफ़ करें = excuse me; मुझे थोड़ा काम करना है। = I need to do a wee wee

I wonder if this is too much? thought Lingo as she added ten spoonfulls of ' बेकिंग पाउडर ' to the mix.

She carefully put everything into the oven and before long,
a sweet cakey smell filled the kitchen.

बेकिंग पाउडर = baking powder

kya hua? yah bahut bada hai!

" क्या हुआ ? यह बहुत बड़ा है !" said Chef.

Lingo realised she had added too much baking powder.

"Sorry," she said sheepishly.

क्या हुआ? = what happened?; यह बहुत बड़ा है = it is huge

They somehow got the cake out of the oven but ...

it was so big ...

... they couldn't hold it. "Disaster!" cried Lingo. " आपदा !" wailed Chef.

आपदा = disaster

"I know what will make you feel better," said Lingo, kindly. 'Eat this ' खीरा kheera '. "

ghinauna. mujhe kheere se napharat hai.
" घिनौना। मुझे खीरे से नफरत हैं ," said Chef.

They were running out of time.

खीरा = gherkin/cucumber; घिनौना = disgusting; मुझे खीरे से नफरत हैं = I hate gherkins/cucumbers

"I've got it! Gunther loves hats, so let's turn the cakey mess into a hat cake! " said Lingo.

First she shaped the cake, then she filled balloons with icing.

Next came the best part: POP! POP! POP!

It was a messy job but in the end, the cake looked fantastic.

laal, naarangee, peela, hara, neela. zabaradast

" लाल, नारंगी, पीला, हरा, नीला। ज़बरदस्त !" said Chef.

लाल = red; नारंगी = orange; पीला = yellow;
हरा = green; नीला = blue; ज़बरदस्त = awesome

There was a knock at the door.

"दरवाजा !" said Chef.
daravaaja

It was Gunther, and he was wearing his special hat!

"Thank you. This makes me feel so special," said Gunther. "You are special," replied Lingo.

दरवाजा = the door

Gunther was thrilled with his cake.

aapako janmadin kee shubhakaamanaen..

Chef's deep voice sang " आपको जन्मदिन की शुभकामनाएँ ..."

आपको जन्मदिन की शुभकामनाएँ = Happy birthday to you

" फूंको^{phoonko} !" said Chef.

Gunther blew out all the candles in one puff and everyone tucked in.

फूंको = blow

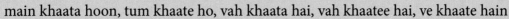

main khaata hoon, tum khaate ho, vah khaata hai, vah khaatee hai, ve khaate hain

" मैं खाता हूँ, तुम खाते हो, वह खाता है, वह खाती है, वे खाते हैं ," laughed Chef.

ham khaate hain

" हम खाते हैं " added Lingo proudly.

मैं खाता हूँ = I eat; तुम खाते हो = you eat; वह खाता है = he eats;
वह खाती है = she eats; वे खाते हैं = they eat; हम खाते हैं = we eat

Everyone was happy.

main khush
" मैं खाता हूँ

tum khush
तुम खाते हो

ham sab khush hain
हम सब खुश हैं ," cheered Chef.

मैं खाता हूँ = I am happy; तुम खाते हो = you are happy;
हम सब खुश हैं = we are all happy

Baking a cake, helping a friend,
learning a new language ... what a day!

But now it was time for bed. It was time to dream
about all the fun things that might happen tomorrow.

Learning to love languages

An additional language opens a child's mind, broadens their horizons and enriches their emotional life. Research has shown that the time between a child's birth and their sixth or seventh birthday is a "golden period" when they are most receptive to new languages. This is because they have an in-built ability to distinguish the sounds they hear and make sense of them. The Story-powered Language Learning Method taps into these natural abilities.

How the Story-powered language learning Method works

We create an emotionally engaging and funny story for children and adults to enjoy together, just like any other picture book. Studies show that social interaction, like enjoying a book together, is critical in language learning.

Through the story, we introduce a relatable character who speaks only in the new language. This helps build empathy and a positive attitude towards people who speak different languages. These are both important aspects in laying the foundations for lasting language acquisition in a child's life.

As the story progresses, the child naturally works with the characters to discover the meanings of a wide range of fun new words. Strategic use of humour ensures that this subconscious learning is rewarded with laughter; the child feels good and the first seeds of a lifelong love of languages are sown.

OVER 50 languages now available! From French to Polish, and MANY MORE!
www.neuwestendpress.com

You can learn more words and phrases with these hilarious, heartwarming stories from NEU WESTEND — PRESS —

LEARN 50 HINDI WORDS

THE FABULOUS LOST & FOUND

AND THE LITTLE MOUSE WHO SPOKE HINDI

WRITTEN BY MARK PALLIS

ILLUSTRATED BY PETER BAYNTON

NEU WESTEND PRESS

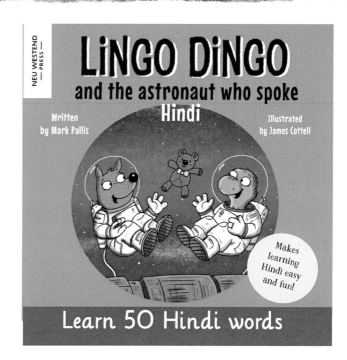

NEU WESTEND — PRESS —

LiNGO DiNGO
and the astronaut who spoke Hindi

Written by Mark Pallis

Illustrated by James Cottell

Makes learning Hindi easy and fun!

Learn 50 Hindi words

CERTIFICATE

Dear _____

Congratulations

You are learning a new language.

You are a **star!**

With my best wishes

Lingo

NEU WESTEND — PRESS —

@MARK_PALLIS on twitter
www.neuwestendpress.com

To download your FREE certifcate, and more cool stuff, visit
www.neuwestendpress.com

@jamescottell on INSTAGRAM
www.jamescottellstudios.co.uk

> "I want people to be so busy laughing, they don't realise they're learning!"
>
> Mark Pallis

Crab and Whale is the bestselling story of how a little Crab helps a big Whale. It's carefully designed to help even the most energetic children find a moment of calm and focus. It also includes a special mindful breathing exercise and affirmation for children.

Featured as one of Mindful.org's 'Seven Mindful Children's books'

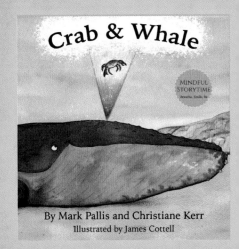

Do you call them hugs or cuddles?

In this funny, heartwarming rhyming story, you will laugh out loud as two loveable gibbons try to figure out if a hug is better than a cuddle and, in the process, learn how to get along.

A perfect story for anyone who loves a hug (or a cuddle!)

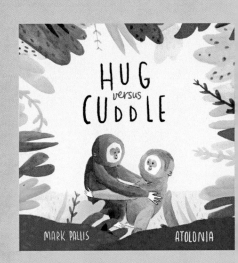

www.markpallis.com

Made in the USA
Las Vegas, NV
17 October 2024

97018055R00024